TRUTH

The Art of Raising Stable Stylish and Secure Children

"A Single Parent Playbook for Success"

Nicole Randle MSN RN

Unless otherwise noted, all Scripture quotations are taken from the Holy Bible 2010, 2019 All rights reserved.

Cover design and formatting by BookBaby Publishing

Print ISBN: 978-1-09835-042-0

eBook ISBN: 978-1-09835-043-7

Printed in the United States of America on SFI Certified paper.

First Edition

Dedication

This book is dedicated to my late mother, who instilled values, morals, and a belief system that all things are possible, which contributed to my assertive, inspiring, and caring attitude. My late father, who expressed the importance of self-care and cared for me unconditionally. Because of their commitment to me as their child and by raising me with a balanced platform I am forever grateful.

Acknowledgment

I would like to acknowledge my children, who are incredibly loyal, supportive, and equally loving. My siblings, those who served as my village of support, my family and spiritual leaders.

Contents

Dedication   v

Acknowledgment   vi

PREFACE   viii

Chapter 1: The State of Being Secure   1

Chapter 2 :Where Is Home   5

Chapter 3: Parents Sometimes Leave   9

Chapter 4: A Child Desire   14

Chapter 5: Your Parenting Style   17

Chapter 6: Are You All In   21

Chapter 7: Build a Life of Purpose   25

Chapter 8: Single Fathers   29

Chapter 9: Spiritual Perspective   32

Chapter 10: Mom Your Parents Were   36
Responsible for Your Childhood

Chapter 11: Create Your Own Environment   39

Chapter 12: You Chose My Parent   42

Chapter 13 Love Is Not Action   44

Chapter 14: Mom You Are Not the Wife   47

Chapter 15 Literacy Matters   51

Chapter 16: Let Your Haters Hate   55

PREFACE

I recall feeling nervous and excited at the thought of becoming a new parent. The reality of having my first child was imminent. The responsibilities would last a lifetime, the experience would be one the child would reference as the years go by. It was necessary to create a bond with my children; while gazing into their eyes, watching their little expressions and personalities, thinking of how to be everything they would need me to be—while understanding my actions or failed actions would impact their lives and forever. Besides, through the eyes of a child they must become familiar with parents, family, and a host of friends with whom they would encounter through this journey called life.

Those moments allowed a foretaste for self-reflection, to evaluate myself physically, mentally, and emotionally. It was clear my decisions would have an immediate impact on those closest to me. In comparison, the family unit of the past consisted of grandmothers and mothers who loved their children/families unconditionally. Those matriarchs provided a pathway even when the fathers were not present which often modeled the epidemy of strength.

Unfortunately, today our foundations are weaker, we are losing our children all in which disrupts the family unit. Single-parent homes are more prevalent, resulting in latchkey children raising themselves along with peers and societal influence. The schematics of financial and socioeconomical disadvantages will never be totally eradicated.

Social media and reality television portray everyone as their best self. However, I caution one not to be consumed with the images, instead, love yourself by creating the picture you would like to see. Interrogate your reality by evaluating the persons within your village. The impossible now become possible when you decide to preserver despite life difficulties, challenges, or disappointments.

Learn to celebrate your achievements, make good memories of those exciting moments as they occur, TRUTH is *The Art of Raising Stable, Stylish, and Secure Children* is not all about finances rather the creation of a solid foundation. Securing all hands-on deck attitude, providing emotional support, creating financial stability, and establishing an authentic village of individuals who support your vision is necessary.

As you progress through the readings, allow time for self-reflection and if there are feelings of discouragement, inadequacies or resentments now is time to forgive yourself. Perhaps you dreamt of a particular lifestyle well do not be discouraged; rather, stay encouraged, as dreams do come true only if you do the work.

The Success of Raising Stable, Stylish, and Secure Children is reflected in those whose lives you have impacted through the many sacrifices. The success is achieved through your decision to provide a solid platform nurturing, demonstration of love, and your commitment. TRUTH is *The Art of Raising Stable, Stylish, and Secure Children* is a marathon, not a race and depending on the outcome of the marathon will also reflect your legacy.

Chapter 1: The State of Being Secure

Joshua 1:9 "Have I not commanded you? Be strong and courageous. Do not be afraid; do not be discouraged, for the Lord your God will be with you wherever you go".

According to Merriam-Webster, the meaning of security is the quality or state of being secure freedom from danger: safety and freedom from fear or anxiety. Abraham Maslow acknowledged the need of protection as a basic human need in his "Hierarchy of Needs."

Safety needs represent the second tier in Maslow's hierarchy. Those needs include the security of body, employment, resources, the morality of family, and health. It is believed a parent executes a pivotal role as the parent seek to provide a safe environment free from hurt, harm, danger, fear, and anxiety.

A significant component of parenting is understanding the importance of those formative and nurturing years from birth to eighteen. A child's role is to play and be delighted. If an environment solicits chaos and confusion, a child may exhibit isolation and lack of interaction with peers or lack emotional attachment. According to Erickson, the stages of Psychosocial Development, Trust vs. Mistrust is successful in infancy if the child develops essential trust from the mother. The first stage is the most critical stage from birth to one year old.

Developing trust and reliability is paramount, followed by confidence which promotes a level of self-esteem to aide in sound decision making skills. Although, trust is learned over time it is not automatic. A child's trust is further enhanced over the years. Securing trust is the act of being present with a safe and secure environment and if successful, trust will last through the various developmental stages.

However, trust may also be easily broken by poor decisions, destructive behaviors, mistruths, or failure to act in a righteous manner. As the mother, have you proven to be trustworthy? Is your child able to solely depend on you or do you defer the child to grandparents to raise? Are you building confidence or fear within your child? Lastly, are you accountable? If not ask yourself why?

What we do today is embedded in a child's memory and psychological makeup which also influence self-analyzation in the future. Failure to create a thriving environment may lead to a child inability to express feelings, lack of emotions towards others, periods of loneliness, creation of imaginary friends, intermittent acts of selfishness; some become shy others are introverted.

As a parent, try to create stability in daily routines, be consistent in decision making, take ownership, to provide your child a sense of safety and belonging. Security is built through sharing, listening, and effective communication with your child. Building a whole relationship is a lifetime journey that requires a lifetime commitment. The formation of this relationship is an ongoing experience throughout the child's life. Understanding how to have positive interactions with others is a good sign of a healthy relationship.

If you are fortunate to be a stay-at-home mom; it is proven that stay-at-home parents have tremendous success with their child because of the extra time spent with the child, allowing both the parent and child to bond.

Should you work outside of the home, a caretaker may be necessary to provide care for the child depending on the age. One way to promote consistency is by allowing the child to remain with the same caretaker or day-care center until the child is ready for school. This may minimize anxiety and repetitive patterns of consistently building relationships with different people.

Although, COVID-19 pandemic has altered the landscape of education, as the parent decide which method works best for you. If necessary, develop a routine with the day-care staff and owner to become familiar with the establishment and set your expectations.

If your child is in school, volunteer to be a room mom which allows the development of relationships with other parents and teachers. By demonstrating interest in your child's future, teachers will also be interested. Some parents now work from home which again has advantages and disadvantages. Although convenient this may not be most suitable and requires implementation of work life balance. The advantages of a stable home environment allow development of building self-esteem, confidence, and autonomy in a child. Have you considered those primarily influencing your child?

TRUTH The Art of Raising Stable Stylish and Secure Children is to keep in mind most behaviors are learned behaviors. Are you your child's greatest influence.

Chapter 2 : Where Is Home

Psalms 113:9 "He gives the barren woman a home, making her the joyous mother of children".

It is a joy when a child knows where home is having a permanent place of residency creates a sense of security. In contrast, the opposite occurs, such as insecurity and instability especially when a parent is constantly changing residence. Consider this each time you change residence places the child at a disadvantage and may give rise to a child's inconsistencies and discontentment of the childhood experience.

Unresolved patterns become the new norm for a child who will undoubtedly manifest the same behavior in adulthood. I understand people change residency for various reason. However, I am speaking in regards, to a pattern of simply changing residence every six months simply because the lease is up, or you are competing with others, or perhaps your parents portrayed a similar pattern of disruption.

The act itself is selfish and will create a feeling of displacement within a child. Try to remove yourself and think objectively as to what this means to your child each time this occurs. The child may need to change schools, make new friends and just about when they are comfortable you are moving again. This repetitive cycle becomes viscous. Whereas having a permanent place to reside is essential, the creation of a space specifically for a child is paramount; it is proven, a safe space is a powerful place for a child.

An established residence means one set of rules which alleviate confusion for the child. Whereas, when a child is continuously moving or residing with different people in different spaces challenges will arise. The child may not understand who rules supersede, and from the eyes of a child, should I listen to my mother today, or should I listen to Ms. Smith because we reside in her home?

A mother's role is to guide, adhere to structure, and nurture, while the father role is to provide and protect. However, in a single parent home, the custodial parent usually overcompensates for the absentee parent. Liken it to a tree. When a tree is planted, watering the tree helps it grow. As it develops, the bark of that tree gets stronger and stronger. Even during a storm, a tree may wave side to side, but it can withstand the storm because it is rooted with a solid foundation.

A stable home environment gives a child a chance, one set of rules, schedule for chores, bedtime, and other activities within the home. This now mean everyone will understand their role(s). In my home, my children were assigned chores on a rotational basis which included general cleaning of the common areas and each were individually responsible for their bedroom.

The remaining of the home was the sole responsibility for me as the parent. I did not rely on my children to clean up after me. As the years progressed a different life skill was taught some things were repetitive relating to chores and activities of grooming. A general rule to cleanliness is that "everything" has a place. Each night, the kitchen was cleaned, swept, and lightly mopped to ensure our home remained clutter-free and clean.

Perhaps, you are not a fan of organization I encourage you to consider developing a routine that is proven to benefit you as the parent as well as the child. Simply put, your son is not to assume the responsibilities of a father. Your daughter is not to assume responsibilities of a mother. Allow a child to be a child by not giving them too much too soon, including responsibility. Allowing a child a chance to gain understanding, grow, and learn those fundamental tasks during each developmental stage is significant and creates wholeness internally.

TRUTH is The Art of Raising Stable Stylish and Secure Children suggest a foundation is necessary. Are you rooted? Have you created a solid foundation for yourself or your child? Interrogate your reality; now you are aware of the consequences of dysfunctional patterns of not being rooted, are you ready to change?

Chapter 3: Parents Sometimes Leave

"You teach people how to treat You."

Parents leave for numerous reasons related to the fear, responsibility, lack of finances; perhaps, they were abandoned, lacked emotional support, a pure act of selfishness, domestic violence, death or maybe addiction influenced the decision. Some parent leave when the custodial parent makes it so difficult for the absentee parent to co-parent.

Nevertheless gone is gone and although there are many excuses there is no justification for removing your parental presence from a child. When a parent leaves, one parent now becomes both parents, consumed with the extra responsibility, often overwhelmed, and plagued by numerous stressors, which may include but not limited to a lack of education, poverty, lack of finances all in which leads to displacement and in an extreme case low self-esteem which often leads to depression.

Most times, people are stressed because they are trying to obtain things well beyond their reach, living beyond the financial means in which you can afford. I urge parents to stop trying to live vicariously through others, stop competing with a grandiose lifestyle and learn to be comfortable with those things in which you were given. Take the pressure off, people do not know what you have unless you tell them.

Are you reaching for something that was never meant to be? Are you competing with someone else's lifestyle? Your desire to be competitive by comparing yourself to others is not true happiness and not emotionally healthy. I am not saying settle, but I am saying be realistic.

When a parent leaves understand people sometimes run away and a runner runs from everyone; they are passive aggressive, cannot resolve problems and blame everyone else for their failure. The role of the custodial parent is to protect the child by helping them understand the absent parent decision was their choice and their choice alone. Ensure the child has the right outlook whatever was taught or not taught is embedded in the child mind during the formative years.

Abandonment is real, and the results are long-lasting. Once a parent has abandoned a child, they will carry this burden of fear with everyone they encounter especially this impacts all types of relationships. Generally, the abandoned child rarely overcomes the fact that a parent left; especially if the custodial parent also exhibited toxic behavior.

A child will spend a lifetime seeking validation, love, acceptance, and the parental relationship with the absentee parent. A parent absence can never be recaptured. It is impossible to recapture birthdays, special school occasions, and a host of other memories. I often tell people stop expecting something from people that they cannot give you and be thankful for the parent that was able to provide your needs.

Perhaps, God was protecting you all along. God's redirection if often his protection. The results of abandonment in a child are a life-long pattern of dysfunctionality. Unfortunately, when a parent leaves a child may exhibit the same pattern when they too become a parent. In some cases a child may decide to be a better parent to their child than their parent was in their own lives.

If you are the absentee parent, I challenge you to self-reflect and identify where the breakdown in the relationship with your child occurred. Were your parents absent in your life? Interrogate your reality are you a runner? Area you a runner or prefer to solve problems? Do you lack emotional support or play the victim so everyone can feel sorry for you?

In most cases the absentee parent will returns when a child is older and no longer co-dependent. This does not mean people will not change; it does not mean people will not desire to do things differently, but it takes a tremendous effort and self-work to change a person behavior. As a woman, let me apologize on behalf of all men who decided to become an absent parent; I apologize to the mothers for those men who took advantage of your heart for general pleasure so you can release and be the best parent to your child.

Likewise, fathers, let me apologize for those absentee mothers who relinquished their rights to nurture, support, and care for their children, those who took advantage of your heart for general pleasure so you can release and be the best parent to your child.

I became a single parent due to the untimely death of my children's father. As the parent. this was a pivotal time, the decision to lead my family in healing was the goal. I refused to allow anyone to create a climate of disruption because of the impact on everyone. The healing process is timeless; yet I remained committed. If we were going to do good, we did well together. If we were going to do bad, we would do bad together; wherever I resided is also where my children resided. Nothing or no one came before my children's well-being.

I was present, sacrificed my time, participated in all school activities, celebratory moments, and provided spiritual guidance. Because I decided to create a solid foundation instead of running from a painful situation. The image was to teach my children how to handle grief and determine the next course of action to continue functioning although you may not be healed by understanding choices have consequences.

Besides having a mother who loved me unselfishly taught me how to be strong despite the naysayers—it taught me how to seek spiritual guidance when problems seemed bigger than life itself, and most of all I understood it is okay being alone. I live by those concepts even today.

TRUTH The Art of Raising Stable Stylish and Secure Children is to realize your child will handle problems the same way you do. You are teaching your child how to handle adversity, pain, and life disappointments. During this time, you decide if you both will win together and lose together.

Chapter 4: A Child Desire

Jeremiah 29:11 "For I know the plans I have for you declares the Lord".

B ecause a child is so precious and fragile, this reminds us as a parent how we should protect and defend them in every way we can. A child is God's chosen vessel; there is a plan for each child's life. God chose the child's parents; they are the children God has graciously given you. I do not know of one child who says, "I want to be nothing when I grow up, or I want to be a loser." A child's dream may be distorted by those closest to them; sometimes, it is the parents. A child desires love, seek time, discipline, structure, and protection.

Sometimes you may think you know people who appear to have good morals or values, but it is important to evaluate the people that partake in your child's life. Do not assume a person character based on what they say because they could say all the right things. Instead, spend time with individuals to determine if their actions equal a favorable behavior, belief system and temperament aligned with your vision. Perhaps you have entrusted a sister, mother, or female acquaintances to spend time with your child and you discover they are teaching your child how to be manipulative, cunning, and deceptive for all the wrong reasons.

There is a great chance your child will manifest the same behavior at some point in life. You are what you hang around. Likewise, there are good women who serve as mentors and will teach our young ladies how to be their best self, maintain respect, be smart, kind, gentle and courteous.

We must also monitor our young men, and not assume a brother, father or close friend will not attempt to derail them. If the wrong male influence surrounds your son this may also derail the child from a life of success. Likewise, there are also male role models who will impart wisdom and teach son's how to be respectful, generous, build self-confidence and not criticize our men. The power of spoken words has life in a child's mind forever as the mother have you spoken blessings our curses in your child's life?

For example, I vividly remember being in Girl Scouts at the tender age of five. I enjoyed Girl Scouts and was in awe of my troop leader. In my eyes, she was smart, well spoken, and often shared history with us. Ms. Jackson was always neat and savvy. I recall the scout meetings, but what I appreciated most was her positive influence. Because of her, I made sure I was also neat, clean, and well-groomed. My scout leader favored me out of many because of my presentation.

Who is shaping your child's perspective? My mother was instrumental in shaping my perspective with style, class, and a home environment reflective of who she was as a person but most of all as my mother. My mother greatest influence was to ensure each of her children pronunciation was tactful. You see a child learns through repetitive action as a matter of fact a child is eager to learn new things and it is your responsibility to teach them. Keep in mind, you are also teaching your child how to treat you. Whatever you do or have failed to do will manifest in your child, if not all your children. Be prepared to provide your child with your best and not someone else's best.

Allow the child to experience you and not who you are pretending to be or competing to be or comparing to be. Who are you or do you allow others to tell you who you are? If you are not able to explain it. There is a strong possibility your child will have the same broken concept.

TRUTH is Raising Stable, Stylish, and Secure Children takes a lifetime of teaching, praying, and support. Do not allow other people to define you. You define yourself and make sure others respect and appreciate who you are.

Chapter 5: Your Parenting Style

Proverbs 22:6 "Train up a child in the way he should go even when he is old, he will not depart from it".

U nderstanding parenting styles will aid in the relationship with your child. There are four types of parenting: The permissive parenting style where the parents do not want to upset the child; the child is the boss, expectations are low, and rules are lenient with little to no strictness.

Second is the uninvolved parenting style where the child is their parent's boss; the parent is often absent, neglectful, passive, or entirely uninterested in being a parent. Authoritarian-parenting is where the parents-know-best approach emphasizes obedience; this type of parent refuses to allow the child to have any input. the parent assumes total power over the child.

Finally, we have the Authoritative parenting style where there is a blend of caring structure and consistency. This type of parenting allows a child to learn how to be assertive, flexible, responsible, and responsive. The parent creates a relationship where clear standards and behavior expectations exist. This is the most effective parenting style where academic success, social development, emotional attachment, and behavioral success occurs.

A parenting style may be adopted from generation to generation; there is no one size fits all. Parents must take time to develop a style and that works best for the family. In general, one becomes the parent that your mother or guardian was to you. In extreme cases are those parents with narcissistic characteristics unknowingly, a child will develop similar characteristics because people do what they see, you are your circle of influence and parents you are your child's experience.

My parenting style best assimilated as an authoritative parent, allowing open communication not negotiation. By maintaining safety and a caring attitude and by encouraging the child to talk freely. I could tell by the look in my children's eyes as to how their day was spent. If there were details to share, parents allocate time for those discussions. Allow the child to have your undivided attention by simply listening. Parent's must be consistent this will be one additional tool to declare success. As the parent remain in control of the situation or issues as they arise, demonstrate to the child how to think through problems and how to resolve problems.

Be consistent in this area remember if you were successful in the early stages of Trust vs Mistrust the child is relying on you as the parent to resolve the conflict or not. For example, your child has an issue in school teach them, to bring those concern to you for a resolution. As the parent this is one of many tests from a child's perspective. They are watching to see how the conflict will be resolved. Are you able to resolve the issue without the child's involvement? You are teaching the child conflict resolution. I encourage you to develop a parenting playbook for success and stick to it. Your playbook will be different from others but it yours, so you guard and protect it.

I speak in great details regarding education because a child enjoys learning, as the parent be involved while enabling the child to also be involved throughout the entire educational journey. Being involved during the formative years, of early childhood education and throughout the college experience is based on an environment that encourages and cultivates education. Parental expectations may be set, the standards to achieve must be clear and together you both will make it happen.

By understanding your parenting style will benefit the entire household or family unit. You adjust as the child gets older because a child needs will change through the course of time. Parenting is a privilege this is your role. You will always be the parent, not a friend the responsibilities are serious-minded and one the parent must demonstrate effectively. Perhaps you are lost and simply do not understand where to begin. Perhaps you desire to break old patterns you must first change the way you "think".

It is my hope you develop the skills to adopt an authoritative style of parenting. Inspire your child to think about consequences of their action, the impact on the family, how to think big, be innovative, be creative, to dream, to seek approval only from those who matter, and as the parent you provide a safe, positive environment, allow for moment of positive reflections stand with the child in all righteousness while correcting all the wrong behavior.

If there are areas in which you would like to improve yourself than begin today. Prepare your own destiny and believe in yourself, yes, it is possible to do more than one thing at one time. Perhaps, your dreams were delayed well it is never too late to try again, but please do not to live vicariously through your child; or become a dream killer you will risk pushing them away.

TRUTH is The Art of Raising Stable Stylish and Secure Children is to remember you are your child's first impression. Your success in parenting requires consistency, in your actions, behavior, thoughts and choices as each decision has lifelong consequences.

Chapter 6: Are You All In

Ephesians 6:4 "Fathers, do not provoke your children to anger, but bring them up in the discipline and instruction of the Lord".

Do you have a healthy relationship with yourself, practice selfcare, take care of yourself mentally, one of honesty? Are you comfortable establishing a healthy relationship with your child? What is the definition of a healthy relationship from your perspective? Are you expecting a performance-based relationship; to simply glorify your child because they make you look good amongst your circle of friends or are you all in? Biblically the word of God has several scriptures surrounding parenting.

When asked, are you all in despite this helps to remove limitations. Some parents are all in depending on the scenario. Now let us consider if the child is gay, are you all in? Perhaps your child is now in adult entertainment, are you all in? What if your child

21

is stealing or has committed some viscous crimes, or suffers with addiction? Are you all in? Sometimes, a parent refuse to be engaged when the child takes the wrong path. I intentionally used worse case scenarios because it is easy to be all in until problems occur.

Yes, most parents enjoy speaking well of their children and sometimes children simply do not make good choices and find themselves in inadequate situations. There are times when a child simply has bad characteristics, but even at that point, as the parent your role is to redirect the child if possible. Remember, during those formative years was the opportunity to instill decent, wholesome characteristic traits and as the child grows remains a chance to further enhance their personality traits.

Now, I am not saying to let a child take you down and deplete you financially but what I am saying is look at what could be done differently. There are times when a parent has done everything to help the child, and the child refuses to follow the guidance by continuing a pattern of self-destruction or being defiant. In cases such tough love may be necessary.

Being all in, requires a discussion and further supports why having sound biblical principles as fundamentals is equally important in a child's upbringing. Successful children are taught to be successful; and in cases where they were not taught by the parent, I am sure there was a person of influence. Being all in means your child success will depend on their efforts. You as the parent will only provide the support through conversation or being the child's role model.

Parent do not attempt to outperform the child, compete with the child, become jealous of the child; this is an early sign that as a parent, you lacked support from your parents in your childhood. This certainly prevents you from being all in and fulfilling your purpose as a parent to the child. Also as a parent if you lack self-identity or perhaps you are not secure in who you are as a person; you may be incapable of being, all in.

Unfortunately, the role as a parent never changes; being a parent does not fluctuate; it is not something one turns on and off at their convenience. If you are not going to be all in and fully committed, the relationship with your child will be challenging. Remember, a parent-child relationship is not based on one feeling. It is okay to demonstrate vulnerability not weakness, this may help the child understand you better. Teach your child how to handle the pressures of life, understand how to keep moving forward despite life challenges, difficulties, by learning how to maintain joy during the best of times or through troubled times this is how you show that you are all in.

Being all in; you stand with your child even when the child decision is not one that you would have wanted your child to make. I recall a difficult time for my son, following college. I understood he made a choice and since choices have consequences for us all. I allowed him to go through that difficult period by himself; my role was to coach, mentor, pray and make sure he remained physically and mentally healthy.

I was all in with my prayers and words of encouragement. I never stopped being a mom I was all in as his confidant, and cheerleader. I was all in by teaching him principles as a black man living in America. Those principles in which he continues to utilize today. The same principles which have led to much of his success. You see I understood how to be all in because I was raised by the most significant person in which was my mother who was always all in. A mother who supported each endeavor loved me unconditionally, covered me with prayers and most importantly she thought it was nothing that I could not do.

Having a mother who believed in me, my ability and was on board through all the success and failures in life. People generally do to others what was done to them.

TRUTH is The Art of Raising Stable, Stylish and Secure Children requires you to go above and beyond the call of duty. By allowing your child to have an experience with you, will result in the child understanding you and a lifetime of memories. As the parent are you building memories of love and laughter or hurt and pain.?

Chapter 7: Build a Life of Purpose

"Purpose is defined as a reason for which something is done, the intention or motive".

Recognizing people can be the best pretenders, and in the right environment, the perfect clown. But when you learn to evaluate people through an honest lens by removing the blinders; their true self may be uncovered. Through this process of discovering takes time understanding your purpose on earth is not about you but what you are willing to contribute to the lives of others. Unfortunately, people live a lifetime and never understand why they exist. Your purpose it is not about manipulating, the misuse or controlling people for your own personal gain. I ask people how they plan to live a life with purpose, they often mention materialistic items; yet those things are meant to be enjoyed but not considered one sole purpose.

Proceed with caution and, stop saying things to sound good, while at the same time, appearing foolish. What do people get when they get you? Do you leave people feeling discouraged? Are those you encounter experiencing a pretender? A person full of big ideas big dreams but no real internal substance. Does the lavish lifestyle you portray only exist on social media platforms? Are you intimidated by people who are smarter than you; so your aim is to constantly devalue them? Tough questions require lots of consideration to intentionally create a moment of self-evaluation as the parent.

Perhaps, your so magical that you hope no one will ever find out the real you. Well each time a person has an encounter with you your character is exposed. Before you can influence a child's life, you must first understand your own purpose but most important your motives and if any of your answers to those questions previously mentioned were self-gain you are not living a purposeful driven life and anything without a purpose is dead.

Perhaps, you are not sure of where to begin, no matter how long it takes, begin by broadening your horizons, evaluate yourself, define yourself do not allow others to penetrate you with negativity by telling you who you are. How would you describe yourself? Think of your strengths those things you excel at, think outside of the norm, do not become stagnant, become familiar with a variety of music genres, indoor/outdoor activities so you can see what your interest are, those things which excite you and adds value your life and others.

Do not be dismayed, because you do not know how to demonstrate what was never demonstrated to you. For example, one of my purposes is to build people through conversation, with acts of motivation and inspiration. The conversation is the relationship, accepting people for who they are and not what you desire them to be. How can you discover what is not discussed?

In earlier years there was no such thing as a life coach's but if you decide to use a life coach, mentor, or confidant to aide in your decision making; you must evaluate the individual to determine if their life reflects the teaching or advice being offer to you. I believe the proof is in the pudding. How can someone teach you if their life is in shambles the purpose of a coach is to not only tell you but live as proof as to what happens when you follow a series of steps.

For example, say, a football coach desire to take you to the super bowl but they never won a game. If a coach has bad credit how can they coach you to have good credit? If they have been divorced several times how can they coach you in having a success-ful marriage? Everyone does not deserve a seat at your table. Who have you given permission to impart words of wisdom in your life?

There is enjoyment in helping others be their best; by serving as a mentor. Mentors inspire a few where a coach inspires many. As an Executive Registered Nurse, the opportunity to enhance the life of others is frequent. Understanding my purpose means I exhibit compassion for others, often seeking an understanding, by determining the best course of action, because people live with hope and by helping others in the right place of mind is an immensely powerful place. Having purpose brings forth the development of relationships, these relationships may be with parents, siblings, children, a significant other, friends or associates. Although each relationship is different, each should add value to your life, and you should add value to those individuals as well.

If you are interacting in relationships without value, you are wasting precious time. I recommend you stop the process and no longer spend time with people who are only in your life to take from you. Do not waste time allowing others to coerce you into bad practices or behaviors where no positive outcome exist. It is okay to spend time alone, it is okay to terminate those relationships where you are not appreciated. Stop going along to simply get along.

The COVID-19 pandemic provided good practice for spending time alone, a time of self-evaluation and especially a time to evaluate those around you. COVID-19 exposed people true selves. Perhaps, you though John Doe was crooked, well the pandemic exposed them. Perhaps you suspected Jane Doe was using you or hustling you. Well the pandemic exposed where you willing to accept those things in which you were seeing? Parents as you build your life of purpose, teach your child to spend time with those who appreciate them as well it; this fundamental principle will empower your child throughout a lifetime.

TRUTH The Art of Raising Stable Stylish and Secure Children is further defined by understanding your purpose, what makes you happy, what makes you excited, and what about you is so unique?

Chapter 8: Single Fathers

Psalm 68:5 "Father of the fatherless and protector of widows is God in his holy habitation".

B eing a single parent is probably the hardest job consumed with multiple responsibilities such as spiritual counselor, nurse, nutritionist, confidant, and protector. In addition a dad must learn to listen objectively and with sensitivity when communicating with a daughter. The father is challenged with understanding the aspects of grooming, appropriate attire, discussion of puberty and dating all in attempt to understand who she will become.

Fathers, a daughter's expectation of a man is based on her reflection of you; Are you a protector, provider or sensitive to her needs? Do you listen to seek an understanding before rendering a decision? Or do you treat your daughter the same way you treat women? If so ask yourself who mis-treated you? If the answer is your mother now would be a good time to seek healing. The only person who can fix a damaged person is the person who damaged them. As the father your child is evaluating you. You have potential unless, the child has labeled the parent as a "messy man." A messy man is a danger to himself and will place you in uncompromising situations. Messy men destroy everything around them and will eventually destroy the relationships with the child and entire family to name the least.

However, for the sake of positiveness, lets focus on those awesome fathers, the fathers raising other men children, those who sacrificed much to provide for their family. I have witnessed several men raise their daughter, and perhaps, they did not understand all the latest and greatest lingo, or technology or have all the updated communication techniques. The farther remained visible responsible and supportive by being present, involved and, while providing financial security

As an aunt I was entrusted with my brother most valuable prize, his daughter because of the positive influence. I understood my role, creating boundaries and maintained respect by asking permission before planning any activities. I never gave the impression that their dad's role as a father was not significant. You see, I was a great aunt because I had great aunts.

Surround yourself single dad's with positive women who will provide positive influences on your son or daughter. Introduce them to ladies who are reflective of what you would like her to become, people of like characteristics. Perhaps you are a single father dating or seeking a wife. I caution you to look beyond the surface, evaluate each prospect and their belief system.

Be honest with yourself, and if you are not seeking a long-term relationship, do not to introduce every woman you meet to your child. The last thing you want to do is create an environment which creates friction and disrupts the household. I am not saying allow a child to take over the home, but I am saying it is essential to understand the people you anticipate adding to the family dynamic.

Fathers let me say, you are not notable for taking care of your child; that is what you are supposed to do. You have the first opportunity to influence your daughter, discuss the importance of being a lady, provide examples as to what they too can expect from a man but most of all, you have the honor of validating her. Once a child is validated, they are prepared for life and will work endlessly to ensure you are proud of them. We recognize many good fathers remain committed to their child and are successfully doing it alone.

TRUTH is The Art of Raising Stable Stylish and Secure Children means whatever you think of your child will determine what your child think of themselves. As a father are you raising a daughter or tearing her apart? Are you raising your son to be a leader or allowing him to only experience your inadequacies?

Chapter 9: Spiritual Perspective

"God created heaven and earth; before His word returns void heaven and earth will fade away."

He is the way, the truth, and the light. God is omnipotent; he is omnipresent and so great that we will never be able to encompass all that he has to offer; he is just that awesome. Personally, living for God is probably one of the most challenging experiences.

People assume they must be perfect to have a spiritual relationship or they can no longer enjoy the finer things of life, which is not true. God desires the weak, wounded and those who are broken. He also is a God of abundance so there is an expectation for those who are believers to experience life in an abundance When you are broken only God can heal, when you are low only God can raise you up. Depending on the experience some people will never return to worship in a church building and because of the COVID-19 pandemic some people have left Christianity all together. There is also a small group of individuals who have rebelled against life as a Christian because of their personal experienced within the church that cause them to question their faith.

A sound stable spiritual foundation means you learn to understand the word of God for yourself trust him and not lean to our own understanding. It is important to walk by faith and believe all things are working together for your good. As a faith-based person there is an understanding that people receive God at different intervals in life, we walk in our divine destiny by understanding who we are as spiritual beings.

If you have made it this far, I encourage you to continue walking by faith, believing in those things which are not in existence and by continuing to move forward on the right track. It is time to forgive yourself for past failures, forgive your parents if they failed you, and begin to add to the playbook of success for you and your family.

It is a biblical principle that you reap what you sow. I assure you the seeds you plant in your child will grow. If you have planted bad seeds those seeds will sprout and grow like weeds. If you have planted good seeds you will reap the harvest, it is only a matter of time. Ask yourself are you planting seeds of fear and codependency, or have you decided to plant seeds of strength, independence, confidence into the child?

Are you afraid of letting go? According to Ecclesiastes Chapter 3 there is a time for everything. It comes a time when a parent must release the child allow them to live and make independent decisions. Scripture says, there is nothing better for people than to be happy and to do good while they live so each of them may eat and drink and find satisfaction in all their toil—this is the gift of God.

Surround yourself with strong-faith people those who may help you and in turn those in which you are able to impart wisdom while developing spiritually. Remove those who pretend to be perfect individuals and include those who are willing to share their testimonies. Understanding in today's time a relationship with God is necessary. Besides how can you love someone in which you refuse to have a relationship with Teach your child how to pray and spend time reading the word of God the Bible is a book that has the process for every aspect of our lives. God say to read and understand the word for yourself.

Ensure you have a spiritual covering of a Pastor or Apostle. God is all-consuming, meaning you must be all in; It is free will but if you never spend time it is just a matter of time when you stop seeking his face. The benefits of living with God certainly outweigh the risks. The reward is your "soul" which will live forever. To those parents who were born with a spiritual gift and function with an anointing, take time to develop a relationship with your child who may also manifest this anointing.

You must take time to nurture the gift? Align with a spiritual leader who teaches you the word of God and not just those feel-good messages. My life excelled to greater heights when I began to embellish in the teaching of my spiritual leader not only was the word taught, but I was also able to read and ascertain a greater understanding. My apostle was fully committed to our congregation during the COVID-19 pandemic. The apostle worked endlessly to ensure the word of God penetrated in our hearts and minds to ease any fear. You see he provided a covering and being obedient to the word of God is a blessing by itself.

I encourage you to pray for wisdom while raising your child, wisdom to remove folly friends, wisdom to have financial discipline, wisdom to know what to say and when to say it, wisdom to know when to encourage and not discourage and wisdom to know when to love and when to let go. A strong spiritual foundation will provide a stable foundation. As you develop your own routine of prayer. I challenge you to start today besides what do you have to lose?

TRUTH the Art of Raising Stable, Style and Secure Children is to consider your role in making the world a better place. Be true to yourself, stop pretending and live-in reality because times have certainly changed the question is have you?

Chapter 10: Mom Your Parents Were Responsible for Your Childhood

Thessalonians 5:16-18 "Rejoice always, pray continually, give thanks in all circumstances; for this is God's will for you in Christ Jesus."

Sometimes people become the parent their parents were to them, which is why I rebuke the myth often spoken which says two-parent homes are the best homes. I know of damaged people as the result of two-parent households. I also know many individuals who were the product of prosperous single-parent households, I am one.

Perhaps, you were raised in lower socioeconomic conditions; maybe no one believed in your ability, so they killed your dreams; perhaps as a child, your parents failed to show you love or support which left you finding your way independently.

Now you are a parent, you can change that; I understand it takes mental work, but the good news is it takes more discipline in general it takes on average of twenty-one days of practicing a new way of doing things to change bad habits. Parents regardless of your past you can begin to create your own environment.

Parents, you are not responsible for the decision your parents imposed upon you, more than likely they reared you in the same manner as their parents. However, you can have a better outcome for your own child by doing things differently and taking on a new perspective.

A good source of healing could begin by sharing your most personable childhood stories with your child this will help the child understand you and accept those things that you cannot change. Break those generational curses imposed on you and your family. Be cautious not to continue the same negative patterns imposed on your life.

For example, if your parent abandoned you as a child, now that you are a parent, it is essential to go back and heal those wounds; if not, the risk of abandoning your child remains. Although, not intentional, people often do what was done to them. It is a revolving door one in which we must assume responsibility. Perhaps, a discussion with your parents or those who contributed to the cycle of pain would begin the healing process. Are you ready for the conversation? It is a process and a commitment that one must be willing to make, or the problem will continue. Therefore, forgive your parents as you learn their story. Also as you heal, it is important not to be jealous of other individuals who may have a great relationship with their parents especially if their relationships are one that you desire to have.

My parents were born during the segregated times, I fortunate to learn my parents had the unconditional love and support of their mothers. Understanding their struggles; helped me understand them. For example, my maternal grandmother had a close relationship with each of her daughters which resulted in my experience of a close relationship with my mother. A relationship I miss now my mother is deceased but one that I will cherish forever.

TRUTH-The Art of Raising Stable Stylish & Secure children helps you reflect on what you are demonstrating to your child? Are you creating a pattern that your child will create one day with you? To understand a person is to understand where they come from.

Chapter 11: Create Your Own Environment

Jeremiah 29:11 "For I know the plans I have for you, declares the Lord, plans for welfare and not for evil, to give you a future and a hope."

In my household, I was the sole decision-maker, encourager supporter, prayer warrior, and confidant. It was essential to create an environment conducive to a reflection of who I was as a parent. The type of parent who was serious regarding finances, savings, education, a natural born leader, full of laughter, one of hope, determination, and faith but lacked patience with people who acted foolish. I established a home where my kids were able to dream an environment where ideas were shared, an environment where we celebrated each other's success and consoled each other in times of defeat.

Together, we created a home where there was peace, harmony, and an understanding that no person was superior to the next.

Everyone within the household was equally valuable we worked together toward individual goals and sometimes goals of the family. There was no time for being idled every moment counted. We explored the world together, by traveling both domestically and internationally, all which helped to shape their understanding of different cultures.

Together, we participated in things that interest each person in the household. It was important to seek an understanding while seeking to be understood as each child required something different of me. Parents create your own environment, despite the trauma you can heal, despite the triggers began to recognize them and triumph. Develop a pattern of reading during the early years introduce books such as Dr. Seuss then progress to self-help books and once a pattern of reading is developed the child is now ready to progress to broader literature while simultaneously expanding their vocabulary.

Discover your own talent and then help your child discover theirs. Again a talent is a gift from God, but what you do with your talent is your gift to him. Create an atmosphere of prosperity by knowing yourself and removing limitations. Perhaps you are saying, "I don't know my talent", well your talent or spiritual gift is determined by what you enjoy doing, the one thing you think about the most, that bring you a smile. For starts think of the top five things you can do without much effort and evaluate each item.

Determine if those things you enjoy inspire others, consider if all else fails would you do the task if you made no money and is it something you know how to do without training meaning the task requires little effort. Your gift is not learned by mimicking others. Work is no longer work when you are operating in your talent.

Help your child discover by creating an atmosphere to promotes creative thinking, develop a forum for conversations surround yourself and your child with people who are achievers those who increase your value, this is not a competition but an opportunity to be better.

TRUTH, The Art of Raising Stable, Stylish and Secure Children to understand greatness is obtained at a cost, the cost involves time, dedication, and a commitment to oneself. I encourage you to remove the millions of excuses and begin operating in your gift by doing so your life will never be the same.

Chapter 12: You Chose My Parent

"Your child; is a reflection of you".

Over time, it has become increasingly alarming the number of parenting relationships which have gone bad for one reason or another. I am grossly concerned when either the custodial parent or the absentee parent devalues one another especially when the child is present.

Most of the time, these discussions lead to chaos and confusion. There is ownership for everyone. It is crucial to stop devaluing the child's parents as it creates a toxic environment, contributes to low self-esteem of the child, and as the child gets older, they begin to look at the parent who criticized the absentee parent differently.

Remember, do your part as the parent; silence has a voice, a child is not a child forever and the one thing a person cannot take from a child are their memories. For example, suppose a parent speaks ill against the father by telling the child, "You're just like your daddy, you're stupid like your daddy, you're dumb just like your daddy, or I cannot stand your daddy; he is trifling," which may be true but please remember words have life and what you speak may come to pass but more obviously, "You" chose the father.

You selected him to be your child's father, so if anyone needs to be criticized, perhaps now would be a great time to perform a self-reflection or self-analyzation exercise to understand what inside of you was attracted to this type of individual. I have witnessed multiple siblings playing against each other, picking and choosing whose dad is the best dad or whose mother was the best. This is further exaggerated when the parent shows favoritism toward a specific child. You noticed I did not say father because, in the eyes of a child, they seek validation from the mother first. If you want to do better, then do that, as doing so will give your child a chance. Help your child develop an objective lens, explain the intricate stages of life but understand you are not a subject matter expert. Regardless as to how you feel about their parent be prepared because the child will love that parent even in their absence.

Parents, be intelligent, not intimidating your child will thank you later. If the absentee parent is no longer in your child's life embrace the decision of the absentee parent by moving forward in a positive way give. DNA cannot be changed; what is in the blood is in the blood, be wise on whom you decide to bear children with; the joy of having a child is a very delicate process and one which requires lots of consideration.

TRUTH The Art of Raising Stable Stylish and Secure Children is to learn when people leave let them go!!!

Chapter 13 Love Is Not Action

Philippians 4:19 "My God will supply every need of yours according to his riches in glory in Jesus Christ."

Love is not an act, rather a demonstration of kindness, support, peace, compassion, understanding, time, planning, and investment. Love is tolerance and patience. Are you willing to stand through the test of times, those good or bad? You will be tested, which is when unconditional love is demonstrated. Love is not a feeling. As a parent, loving the child does not equate to trickery or misguiding or simply buying the child material things.

People demonstrate their love for you, the way they care for a vehicle, a favorite pair of shoes, apparel, or blanket. As a parent, if you love your child, provide for your child, and stop soliciting a reward for doing what you should do. There is no trophy for being responsible. According to Erik Erikson, a psychologist theory of psychosocial development, identified, Intimacy versus Isolation as one of the eight stages.

The major conflict centers on forming intimate, loving relationships with other people. Successful completion of this stage in life results in happy relationships and a sense of commitment to self. Loving yourself allow others to love you. If you are not happy with self or lack self-love this does not constitute failure unless you refuse to address the underlying issue.

It is all about remaining connected, and if you are going to be a parent, you must be 100% connected; should you decide to be disconnected understand when you are older the child will disconnect from you. It is true your life is not your own once you have a child. I have never seen a person be successful without putting in the effort plus time. Perhaps you are saying I do not know how to do what was never done to me, or no one ever expressed love to me or told me something positive about myself—well that is okay.

First, start by deciding to move forward providing unconditional love in an atmosphere that allow your child to be honest and share the most intricate details of themselves. Also nurture your sons, a mother's love for her son is priceless; There is a myth that says mothers cannot raise a young man to be a man, but a mother can demonstrate to a son how to love, appreciate, and respect our daughters.

As parents we are responsible for building self-esteem and confidence in our children. A son will respect a young lady based on his interactions with his mother. Parents love your child by protecting them. I once witnessed a man instructing a two-year old to be a man; a two-year-old is still a baby. Mothers stop allowing the destructive behaviors of others penetrate the lives of your child.

Prepare your son to be a leader, but do not insight fear, insecurity, or emotional abandonment all in which prohibits the child from achieving all that life has to offer by giving the child a chance. Love them unconditionally, practice being a good listener even if you do not have the answers, provide credible advice and daily encouragement. Love enhances a child mental well-being, increases physical health, creates a strong bond, also makes your child well rounded. Once you know better, you can do better,

TRUTH is The Art of Raising Stable Stylish and Secure Children will be your playbook. Have you been tested tried and proven for success?

Chapter 14: Mom You Are Not the Wife

Psalms 115:14 "May the Lord give you increase, you and your children."

As a mother raising a son alone is not easy. The child will one day become a young man and although you may see them as you little man, there comes a times you must let them go while you see them evolve into a well-esteemed man and one day someone husband. Letting go may be difficult, the transition may take you a long period of time; but it must occur.

Oftentimes when a father is not within the home a young man feels obligated to protect their mom, while providing financially, especially when obstacles exist and in turn the mom, if not careful, will become co-dependent, and in some sense feel entitled. The sacrifice of the child is enormous in some instances this additional responsibility means time participating in childhood activities and socialization with peers are missed because of obligations to help the family unit.

Depending on the length of time a mother may become so attached and refuses to relinquish the co-dependency their actions become territorial and often aggressive to assassinate the child's relationship with others. Mothers, you are not your son's wife, and you will never be a candidate in the role of a wife. Cut the cord, otherwise the onset of a very controlling dominating personality, manipulative tactics, and your selfishness will be visible to others and disrupt the family unit.

Are you the type of parent who finds a problem with everyone the child encounters? Are you best with manipulative tactics to be a damsel in distress for the sole purpose to have your son provide for you? This may be an act of fear because the environment once created is now changing.

Instead, mom be thankful your child was willing to help during a time of need. Understand the child's role is not to be a parent or sole provider of the household. I understand financial constraints may occur where a child may help by having a part-time job, but you should never intend for your son to assume the role as your husband or create such a perception.

A child grows up and if you love them, apologize for the inappropriate behavior, and let them to go. Stop being jealous because your son brings home someone's daughter who is intelligent and smart and now you feel some type of way. You are the person you decided to become right. Allow the connection with your son to be one of joy, not defeat, one of caring and not control, one of sharing and not selfishness. Be proud of the man you raised by allowing him to love someone else daughter and encourage him to do so. Otherwise, the controlling mechanisms will hinder the mother son relationship there may even be resentment.

As the parent search yourself to understand your own insecurities. Love your son but let them go, encourage your son, be available to support them when they have questions, hug them if they are feeling low, reassure them when times are weary. If no one else believes in them, you should.

It is important to know your role and once you know your role understand what is required of you. Then finally, play your role on the team. For example: If you are the quarterback be the quarterback not the kicker. You see it is impossible to play both roles simultaneously. This does not mean you cannot serve as a substitute during certain intervals.

Remember, the role as a mother involves listening, coaching, being excited, encouraging, and nurturing while leading by example. Where, the role of a wife is to be a life partner, console, comfort and provide intimacy. Mom be happy doing you and stop the competitiveness you will never find fulfillment competing with your son wife who may not be competing with you.

You are your own enemy when you do not know your role. So ask yourself why are you so intimidated? Were you taught as a child to feel insecure and inferior? Love is wanting the best for your son by allowing him to live his life and enjoy the benefits of a relationship with a woman he so desires. He will forever cherish you as a mother for loving him and his wife.

Think, have you ever been a daughter in law? If so, how were you treated? Learn to love people at the level you find them. Find a space in your own heart to accept others and be fair. Are you not appreciative, but resentful? Resentful, because perhaps your son will experience a relationship that you long for. It takes comfort and self-esteem to understand what you were created to be.

Be thankful for your new daughter-in-law, learn to love her, love on her parent's; and engage with her family if they allow you to do so. One day you may have grandchildren. How can you love your grandchild and not care about the mother? It does not make sense and it will never make sense to the child. Stop competing with what you should be okay with. Challenge yourself to do better and be a better person than the person who that hurt you.

TRUTH is The Art of Raising Stable Stylish Secure Children is understanding how to love your son and share your son with others.

Chapter 15 Literacy Matters

2 Thessalonians 3:10 "For even when we were with you, we gave you this rule: if a man does not work, he shall not eat."

What is your motive for financial prosperity? Is your motivation inspired because of your desire to impress boast and shun others? I must tell you, if your motives or intentions are not aligned with the principle of reciprocity you will never acquire abundance or financial prosperity. Take a moment and consider your status. I have watched people chase money only to never acquire it. Often, the battle of finances is lost because of the lack the overall discipline.

How you evaluate money is important most are you operating in a poverty mentality, have you spoken a financial curse over your life, perhaps, it is based on your own experience of a generational lack of understanding because the ability to acquire money is neither good nor bad, depending on whose hands you place the money in. Gain does not mean godliness; some of the richest people can be evil, physically sick, or suicidal. However, godliness with contentment is an excellent gain. Oftentimes a person's value or the amount of money one has is determined, by the home one resides in, the number of cars a person has, or the clothes a person own.

In actuality, the people you are trying to impress may not know you or even care. Earlier, we discussed understanding your gift or talent. Your gift will bring financial prosperity to you. Parents are you building an empire with your child aligned with the same principles? The more you chase money, the less you have. Stay focused on your gift, the money will come towards you.

A biblical principle is to give one-tenth of your income back to God. Are you a tither? Can God trust you with the blessing (money), or do you run off with the blessing Do not equate money to materialistic accomplishments, the first sign of financial maturity is not being wasteful in spending, making wise choices and obtaining financial wisdom. Learn to invest begin building banking relationships, stop utilizing pay-day loans and learn to save.

By doing so, will not only increase but multiply that in which you have shared. It is also wise to understand there are no get-rich-quick schemes financial success is achieved through discipline hard work and by partnering with others who are also successful.

Literacy matters regarding education the goal is to remove limitations. Now let me be clear everyone does not have to pursue a college education. We still need electricians, plumbers, landscapers etc. in my opinion all jobs are necessary, and COVID-19 has certainly determined that for each of us.

As a Registered Nurse I am committed to a life-long learner. My children had the freedom of expressing their desires for college choice and career goals. Although, I was clear in the timeline to complete their education I remained committed and supported their dream. Neither child is an accountant or a Registered nurse, my son is a finance guru with an MBA. My daughter, a clinical psychologist with a master's in psychology.

Establishing educational literacy which begin as early as two years of age. This is time to introduce the books, visual-audio, and other educational material which will also aide in understanding the type of learning style your child best identifies with as everyone learns differently and because of COVID-19 learning platforms have also changed.

Each person learns differently which is what make each person so unique. Is your child a visual learner one who enjoys pictures, whiteboards? Are they auditory learners meaning they are good listener, have rhythm and learn best though lectures? Are they a kinesthetic learner one who enjoy using their hands, and learn by doing? Are they linguistic learners who express themselves with the use of words? Are they a logical learner who enjoy numbers and logical thinking? Are they an interpersonal learner who enjoy learning in groups? Perhaps, the child is an intrapersonal learner one who prefers to learn independently?

Engage your child early to create a level of excitement with learning. Learning is fundamental; children enjoy learning and prepare a solid foundation early foundation will prepare the child for optimal achievement. I often hear people say, "I want my child to be better than I was." Well, I ask what you are doing differently. Each day should be a day of learning and engaging. One benefit is to make the subject fun, enjoyable, and explore it with the child. Learning is fun when you take an interest in learning together. Prepare your child a well-rounded future by providing the pathway to help them succeed. I am not saying you set a low expectation for a child. Simply assist the child in deriving long-term goals.

Create an environment where open dialogue exists opposed to an atmosphere of rebellion where a child will fail simply because they are acting out due to parental demands. As a single parent, be intentional teach your child to have a connection with people who have the same energy and attitude to succeed. I encourage you to inspire, motivate and provide the necessary tools to help prepare your child with a strong educational pathway. By having a degree, does not mean you are better than the next person, it does remove barriers and the possibility of being excluded job opportunities depending on the industry.

TRUTH is The Art of Raising Stable Stylish and Secure Children is to help them discover their strengths not weaknesses. Have you taken time to evaluate your child learning style? When you invest in your child's education will ensure the child excel to greater heights.

Chapter 16: Let Your Haters Hate

Matthew 6:33 "But first seek the kingdom of God and His righteousness, and all these things shall be added to you".

Your haters are afraid of the gifts that God has placed inside of you. This is envy and jealousy at its finest; this person simply does not like you. In previous years, a hater would hate from a distance. Well, today haters are much bolder they try to befriend you or sometimes take a special interest in all aspects of you as their goal is to be you. Others compete with you while secretly begrudging you at the same time. These individuals are the best imitators and good with disguise they are energy vampires. They sit low while listening to your ideas pretending to be excited for you.

Parents should not be confused as a form of flattery it is not. The hater recognizes the power you have within to make things happen. The power of your influence towards your family they are specifically zoned into you. Well, let your haters hate either way it is time to cut the cords and suffocate them by removing your physical presence. They may continue to watch you but allow this to occur from a distance. Do not worry it is nothing like being a boss, a well esteemed single parent who has the epidemy of strength, educated, hold multiple degrees, highly skilled, talented, classy, jazzy, stable, stylish, and secure, a boss because you understand your own value and not seeking validation from people who really do not matter.

As you proceed be careful of who you give advice too. In return be careful of the person who is consistently seeking your advice or ideas to defeat you. Perhaps, you are saying how can I recognize a hater I enjoy giving advice? For starters, they will never congratulate you verbally, they will never enjoy celebratory moments with you, and they will never be the initial person to place a smile on your face. Those celebratory moments, or things important to you will be acknowledged the day after the occasion or not at all. Remember their presence in your life is to take and this is by any means necessary.

Let your haters hate because no one took time to invest into their lives. This person is empty, lost and broken eagerly sitting and waiting to either see or hear the next best thing that is happening in your life. Once you understand that you are a TREAT, when you can help, heal and be excited for others. Those who function as a TREAT understand the responsibility of the following.

Teach because you hold the keys to your success and the success of your child. Teach your child not to desire those things in which others may have; only desire those things which belongs to them. Everything is not for everybody. You see in life one should never be haste for anything. The ability to live your own life and not someone else is so significant. Do not be judgmental but it is wise to create barriers, be wise on who you allow in your space. For example withing the basic function of the human cell exists two key areas. The first is the membrane of the cell that regulates what flows in and out of the cell. Secondly, are lysosomes who function to digest anything that invades the cell and get rid the toxic substances. Are you functioning like a cell?

Recognize, when a person has taken your ideas to use toward their own personal gain, continue to help your child identify their positive characteristics, those things which make them unique. Again this is not a comparison to someone else. Understanding their positive attributes will allow them to excel at greater heights. so they can begin to be their best self. Also help your child recognize when a hater is in the circle. They should place a distance and stop the communication with that person immediately. Haters are low vibrational people with negative energy and spend so much time trying to devalue others, who are great in their presence. This is an attempt to assassinate a person character because you are what they wish they could be; and if you are not careful the hater will try to destroy you and your child.

Elevate by praying your enemies away from you, no vengeance, no ill intent but simply remove yourself from them and pray they adhere to another prey. Unfortunately, jealousy is a learned behavior, and if you are a hater, thank whoever in your village, that taught you how to be jealous and envious of others' success. You cannot tear down what you did not build, so let your haters hate because they will never be able to emulate your class, style, self-respect, or the dignity you have for yourself. The hater cannot break you after all, your hater did not make you. Let your presence proceed you as first impressions are lasting impression and know it is okay not to allow people to misuse you, begin today by protecting yourself, and your energy.

Approve and enjoy being your true self validate yourself; be all you can be besides its your life. There is nothing like a well-dressed individual, its true people still judge a book by the cover. In earlier years, the way a person dressed was recognized as an expressive means of social distinction, and often exploited in class warfare to gain leverage. One's style of dress was so significant it became a powerful tool to negotiate and structure social relations as well as to enforce class differences.

See you cannot buy class; some people take a great amount of consideration in the way they dress others simply do not care. Parents teach your child the importance of wearing specific attire at certain times quality does matter. Expose your child to different cultures we live in a melting pot of people understanding how to be sensitive to others is the outcome, expose your child to a fine dining experiences and teach your son's how to pay the bill when dining is complete, developing responsibility is the outcome. Teach your son etiquette, demonstrating courteousness will be the outcome.

Parents teach your daughter the expectation of a man. Understanding a man's treatment must be kind, gentle, and not rough and exhausting. Please understand your relationship with your child will impact how he or she views the opposite sex. If your son has watched you take men to dinner and pay the tab, then he will expect women to do the same.

Time reveals all things learn how to move in silence. When it is time it will happen it is a universal law. Life is all about having an experience, living a life of abundance and not ignorance. We must get back to sharing those special times with our children; yes, a son desires the influence of a father, but they also require nurturing from their mother, by doing so, will give them the tools to provide, protect and respect the ladies with whom they encounter. Yes, daughters need the affection of a father, but the mother serves as a role model. Take time to teach your daughter how to care for her body and maintain her home environment. Money can buy expensive cars, homes, clothes but it cannot buy class. Take time with your child, everything thing has a place. Neatness is a learned behavior, the way a child behaves at home will also be the way they behave in public.

Parents be committed to the appearance of your child, develop a self-caring attitude in during those early childhood years. The activities of daily living include grooming which includes developing a pattern to ensure your child clothes are ironed, clean and color coordinated, groom the hair, develop good dental habits, include yearly physical exams and a well-kept environment as these things will require your time and devotion to the success of your child.

TRUTH is the Art of Raising Stable Stylish and Secure Children requires a life-long commitment of training from you. It is not about your money rather your value system? You see a well-trained emotionally stable child is developed through time love and patience. Are you the TREAT? Because what is solid can never be broken.